Margret and H. A. Rey's

Merry Christmas, Curious George

Written by Cathy Hapka

Illustrated in the style of H. A. Rey by Mary O'Keefe Young

HOUGHTON MIFFLIN HARCOURT
Boston   New York

This is George.

He lived with his friend, the man with the yellow hat.

He was a good little monkey and always very curious.

CHRISTMAS
TREE
FARM

Today George was visiting a Christmas tree farm.

"You can help me pick out the perfect tree for our home," his friend told him. "Keep close to me while we look."

George promised to be good, but little monkeys sometimes forget . . .

The Christmas tree farm had more trees than George had ever seen.

He found a very nice one right away . . .

But then another caught his eye . . .

George could not resist climbing up the tallest tree to get a better view.

He looked for the man with the yellow hat. But his friend was nowhere in sight.

Two men tromped into the clearing.

"There's our tree!" one man told the other.

The men cut down the tree and loaded it onto a truck—

—along with George! George held on tightly. He saw the man with the yellow hat as the truck drove away, but the truck was going too fast. George could not jump off. He was scared, but still a little curious.

Soon the truck stopped in front of a hospital.

George peeked out of the branches as the men carried his tree inside.

The hospital was a busy place.
George jumped out of the tree.

There was lots here to see and do!
He looked at some interesting pictures.

He found a jacket and tried it on.

He played on a trampoline.

He even went for a ride on a speedy little cart. What fun!

Then George spotted something very interesting. His tree!

George knew that Christmas trees were supposed to have tinsel and twinkling lights and shiny ornaments. But this tree was empty.

George thought and thought—and then he had an idea.

Next George noticed a pile of gifts in the corner of the room.

The gifts looked pretty. But George was curious. Could he make them look even prettier?

This red bow would look much better on the green box. And the nametags might look nicer on different packages, too . . .

A nurse arrived, and what did she see? "A monkey! And he's making a big mess!"

A group of children crowded around the nurse. They were all patients at the hospital. Even though it was almost Christmas, the children were not smiling or looking happy.

"Come along," the nurse said, picking George up. "I'd better get you out of here before you can ruin anything else."

A girl with a cast stared at George's tree. Suddenly she giggled. "Look," she said. "It's my x-ray!"

A boy laughed. "And there's the balloon from my room."

All the children started chattering and laughing as they looked at George's funny decorations.

"Can't he stay for the party?" a boy asked the nurse. "We don't mind about the gifts. It will be fun to sort them out."

"Please let him stay! Please!" the other children chimed in.

When she saw how happy the children looked, the nurse looked happier, too. "I suppose he can stay," she said. "IF he promises to help fix the tree!"

George was happy to help. The children helped, too. Some of them returned George's decorations, while others handed George the real ornaments. He scampered up and down, stringing lights and hanging tinsel. Being a monkey, he was good at that sort of thing.

He was also good at making the children laugh.

When the tree was finished, George helped open the gifts. He was
having such a good time that he completely forgot he was lost . . .

. . . until the man with the yellow hat hurried into the room. "There you are, George!" he cried. "I followed that truck all the way here."

George was very happy to be reunited with his friend. The nurse invited them both to stay for milk and cookies.

"Ho ho ho! Did someone mention milk and cookies?"

A man in a red suit walked into the room, his belly jiggling. He was holding a beautiful golden star.

George's eyes widened. It was Santa Claus!

"Who would like to put the star on top of the tree?" Santa asked.

"George!" the children cried at once. "Let George do it!"

George scurried up the tree one last time. He put the golden star in place carefully.

MERRY CHRISTMAS, CURIOUS GEORGE!

www.hmhco.com
www.curiousgeorge.com

The text of this book is set in Adobe Garamond.
The illustrations are watercolor.

ISBN 978-1-328-69558-1
Manufactured in China
SCP 10 9 8 7 6 5 4

4500765593

Manufactured in China 4500656894